Early life

Six months prior to my birth on 14-9-1961 mother of my maternal grandfather had a dream, a Muslim saint Hazrat Banoor Baba originally buried in Bait ul Muqadas Palestine had informed her about my birth and had suggested my name to her repeatedly thrice to make her memorize the name Abdur Raziq. After six months of her dream I took birth in delivery room of Sangirh hospital in Kohat. My mother a girls school teacher at that time within next eight years became a proud mother of three sons and a daughter. I had brought good fortune for the family founded by our eldest ancestor Colonel Guldar Khan of Royal British Indian Army.

Besides prior to my birth family of my grandfather and maternal grandfather during last hundred years were transformed from the pure status of feudal to land owners, businessmen, civil and armed forces servants, and artisans, family riches were reduced to our remaining family property in Kohat Garrison in shape of our family graveyard having shrine of our elder saint Hazrat Nabi Shah Bukhari, rest of our three square kilometer family land was taken over by British colonial rulers in 1923 but after my birth situation was gradually changed and wealth and riches had recovered us again.

Known history of my family on government records begins from 1876-77 here in Kohat district, probably British colonial rulers had started keeping record of families from that year. My Awaan Malyar tribe owner of Charbagh lands situated around five water springs in heart of Kohat city, in known history was headed by Colonel Guldar Khan of royal British Indian Army.

Honorable Guldar Khan had two sons Barkhurdar Khan and Namdar Khan, then Namdar Khan had three sons, Azad Khan, Jalal Khan, and Abdullah Khan.

My family elder Abdullah Khan was having seat in court of British Monarch and he used to visit London to attend royal court there as courtier of British Monarch.

My grandfather Faqir Muhammad Khan was son of Azad Khan. Ghulam Haider Khan, Muhammad Akbar Khan, Muhammad Sarwar Khan, and Muhammad Aslam Khan were real brothers of my grandfather Faqir Muhammad Khan.

During childhood period me and my cousin used to enter safely in main gate of our family residence in presence of two camels sitting there waiting woods to be downloaded from their backs. Main gate was good for entry of two elephants together of our family residence known as Wada Whera (big lawn).

Me and my cousin's residences were separated from main family residence where around 17 families of cousins of my father were residing.

We both used to go to our main family residence to meet our favorite uncles and aunts and to play with our cousins under a huge tree planted by our forefathers in center of big lawn. Now one of my cousin and class fellow Umair has bought our huge family residence in Kohat city and is planning to make market in it.

In a three story building of my ancestral home in Kohat city, my father, grandfather, grandmother, my uncle Mushtaq, Naseer and Muneer, aunt Shakila, their cousins Umar, Yousuf and Haji Muhammad were also living along with their wives and children, at first floor of the building a bedroom was specified for my mother and father, me and my brothers Shabir and Abdur Rauf used to sleep with our grandfather and grandmother in their large bedroom located on second story of the building in our ancestral home. Cousin of my father Umar uncle, his mother, his wife Taj Rihan Aunty and his daughters Bushra, and Bano, son Khayyam and Ahmed, Yousuf Uncle his Wife Aunt Amina and his only son Inam, and his grandma

Fatima, Uncle Haji Muhammad, his wife and two sons and two daughters we were all living together in a joint family system, in the same home.

The most nice place to spend time was Convent School where I got admission in nursery class, prior to my admission in Convent School in Kohat district of Pakistan, I was attending Government Ghula Mandi School, which was located in a building of old Hindu Temple, I was compelled to sit on floor on a mattress with my other class fellows, when my class teacher wearing Karakul cap on his head had kicked me on my back while I was sitting on mattress and trying to read from book, I stood up pulled my school bag on my shoulder and just started walking towards outlet, had reached my mother whom was a teacher in nearby government girls school, I told her straight away, enough is enough my class teacher had kicked me for no reason, cannot attend this school any more, my great mother was angry like a lioness, she said ok you will be admitted in Kohat Convent and will be treated well, she was true my Convent School teacher in Nursery class was an Irish blond Miss Sheila pretty like a fairy, and kind like a mother, Chitrali Princess Miss Cozy and Miss Ann a British national were my seniors in School, among teachers I still remember kind Madam Gulzar, Miss Sheila, Sister Bernadine and Principal mother Helen, kind father Joseph and sister Raphael had played great role in shaping my personality, till class five I was in Kohat Convent, my family finances were suddenly shrunk and my parents were compelled to send me to government school, my cousin Shakir was quite a great help, when I had joined Urdu medium government school, we both were in a same class, a class fellow Rehmat used to come to school on his donkey, he was elder then me, used to sing Pushto songs in class room in absence of teacher, mostly while singing songs he used to look towards me, I was unable to understand Pushto and was worried about his intentions but due to our family background no one had ever dared to inflict any harm on me or my cousin Shakir, as children we both were always focus of attention because of our good appearances, even in college situation was same.

In class seventh, a Mullah Islamic Studies teacher had once virtually lashed me in class room when I had failed to memories a sura from holy Quran, for few weeks I was unable to lay down at my back to take sleep. Soon the Mullah teacher was killed by his enemies in desert of Lachi village of Kohat; his dead body was eventually found and buried.

During my childhood Field Marshal Ayube Khan was ruling Pakistan, in Convent School it was announced that Field Marshal is coming to Kohat students will greet him when he will pass through the road in front of our school, I was also standing there in my school uniform when field Marshal had appeared in black car, his car was moving slowly in front of us, all the school children were clapping with jubilation, for few seconds I became a focus of field Marshal's eyes and he smiled while waving his hand towards me, I waved back and started clapping in jubilation. For few seconds during eye contact with field Marshal I had felt warmth and kindness of his inner self and from that very day when I was just four years old, I became fond of joining Pakistan Army, I have thrice tried to join Pak Army, and twice tried to join civil services of Pakistan but due to my odd circumstances I was unable to succeed.

During two years in Commerce College Kohat, was made unopposed president of student union, had worked for good of my fellow students in that capacity. After 12th grade exam result have joined government college Kohat as third year student. And for masters in International Relations have joined Quaid I Azam University Islamabad in 1982.

University days

Dr Rasool Baksh Raees, Dr Sikander Hayat, Dr. Ijaz Hussain, Dr. Syed Riffat Hussain, Dr Waseem, Madam Aqeela Khwaja, Mr. Sajjad Haider, Dr Parvez Iqbal Cheema, Dr Zafar Cheema, Dr Ijaz Shafi Gailani, Mr. Sher Bahadur, Mr. Rasheed Khalid and Mr. Imran Hameed had taught us during university years, when I had joined Quaid I Azam University Islamabad as student of International Relations in 1982.

Prior to my admission in QAU, I wanted to become a Lawyer, had traveled to Karachi to join SM Law College, had a stay with Mr. Peer Baksh Mehtab and Mr. Arshad for four days, on 1st of January 1982 I received phone call from our family friend Mr. Irshad that my admission is finalized in Quaid I Azam varsity of Islamabad, I reached back to Kohat and then after collecting my bag and baggage reached Quaid I Azam University Islamabad.

When taxi car was reached near hostels of Quaid I Azam University on 4th January 1982, a tall figure had appeared from the mosque near hostels and came smilingly towards me, in Pushto language he had introduced himself as Qassim Marwat from Pak Studies department and had picked my bed on his shoulders, I just followed him, he entered in hostel four and entered in a room along with my bed then he invited me to enter the room, the moment I entered the room I found a bearded person sitting in a chair, when introduction was made I came to know that his name is Zaigham Awan and he is Nazim of Jamiat Tuleba I Islam, in campus he is the boss and distribute rooms in hostels among new comers, he had introduced me with one another person Shehzad who was from Peshawar and was head of hardliners wing of Islami Jamiat Tuleba, Mr. Shehzad had ordered burgers and tea for me in canteen and then came back, meanwhile Mr. Zaigham Awan had kept on talking to me about agenda of Jamiat Tuleba and had tried to convince me to get myself committed with agenda of his party, I smilingly told him finally that I am tired now, need room to adjust myself there and further informed him that I am not interested in politics want to complete my studies, committed with his cause he had smilingly ordered his fellows to break the lock of room no 1 in hostel one, he has told me, the room is already occupied by Mr. Javid a student of economics and worker of his party, whom is gone to his village Narowal Sialkot Pakistan now, I can stay in his room till the time another separate room is arranged for me, I bought a new lock to replace broken one, and had adjusted my luggage in room no 1, its cupboard was already filled with luggage and clothes of Mr. Javid, smell of oil known as local edible oil was spread in the room, no one was available to come up with remedy to this problem, I slept in a smelly room during my first night in hostel, in morning I had reached International Relations department, while standing near notice board to read notices, suddenly I heard a female voice, are you a new comer?

I looked towards her and found unbelievably beautiful girl standing beside me, I replied yes, she said, she is also a new comer, she was wearing gray coat and was elegantly dressed up, had introduced herself confidently that her name is Seema Zakir, and is my class fellow, I told her my name and exchanged few formal words with her, then I had entered in office of the head clerk to get admission fee forms, within half an hour I had deposited my admission fee along with hostel security dues, university administration was headed by vice chancellor Mr. Imtiaz Sheikh, but virtually control in hostels and departments was with Islami Jamiat Tuliba, being a realistic person I had accepted this reality and tactfully managed to get separate room for myself in hostel four within a month, majority of my class fellows were girls, strict professors, strict semester system rules, high standard of education were keeping me and my class fellows round the clock busy.

Hostel life was a new experience for me; I had completed my Bachelor of Arts degree from Government Degree College Kohat a college located in my native city Kohat, during early fourteen years of my education I was living with my parents in Kohat. In Islamabad I was residing in hostel of QAU and had completed my masters in International Relation in 1984 in B grade, had qualified written test for job of producer in Pakistan Broadcasting Corporation but soon I had realized that General Zia was only interested in inducting people having recommendations from Jamaat I Islami leadership, I was rejected in interview by the selectors on a plea that warm suit which I was wearing at the time of interview was quite expensive. After getting rejected by the cronies of dictator Zia I came out from the building of PBC Islamabad and had opted to stay back in home town Kohat, in year 1985 I was remain there in my home town Kohat, had read War and Peace of Tolstoy along with many other books related to International Relations, Dr. Henry Kissinger and President Nixon were always my favorite writers, memoirs of President Nixon were quite interesting, even now I do not miss to read recent writings of Dr. Henry Kissinger.

In August 1986 I was fed up from Kohat and had got admission in M Phil US Study at Area Study Center

of Quaid I Azam University Islamabad, again got a room in hostel no 2 of QAU, life in ASC was tougher

then IR department, no second chance was there in ASC during course work, less than 58% marks during

course work mean ouster as symbol of failure, seven students from NWFP had met failure in the past, I

was the first one from NWFP whom had completed course work.

I used to attend seminars and conferences as column writer during my M Phil course work, I was

encouraged by Professor Khalid Rasheed in 1986, he was working with English daily The Muslim. I used

to write columns on PAK-US relations for daily Muslim. My M Phil Thesis supervisor was Professor Dr.

Sikandar Hayat, the most polished and polite person was appointed as my supervisor, I was feeling lucky,

then came the election year, the dictator Zia was willing to hold elections and was also willing to let PPP

lead by Muhtarima Benazir Bhutto to participate in elections, the old dictator was finally convinced.

US ambassador Mr. Robert Raphael came for a seminar in ASC and during question answer session point

was raised by Madam Faryal Ali Gohar regarding USA's keen interest in forthcoming elections in

Pakistan, and arrival of US observers to monitor the election. Faryal had straight away asked the

ambassador, why you Americans are so nosy? Election is Pakistan's internal affair; we do not need any

US observers. In response to her remarks the ambassador invited us to observe forthcoming US presidential elections as observers.

In humid and hot month of August 1987 General Zia along with US ambassador Raphael and many other high-ranking Army officers was killed in air crash, and Ghulam Ishaq Khan became President of Pakistan. I was working on my M Phil thesis, a senior of mine Dr. Javid from Gujar Khan was a great help in that respect, and he by himself was doing PhD at that time from ASC.

After the completion of course work, I was able to spend some time with my friends and university fellows, Asma Fakhri Abu Talib, Tariq Abdullah, Madhuri Chawla, Nasir Khan, Ishtiaq and Afigee Qassim Ishaq Jee were good friends and university fellows, few dance parties at residence of Asma and few dinners at residence of Madhuri Chawla are the worth remembering memories of the past. Once Children of the employees of Indian embassy in Pakistan came to QAU campus with my Indian friend Madhuri Chawla, her father Mr. Chawla was admin officer in the embassy, the moment I was introduced to the children they had remarked abruptly, you look like god Krishna, later Madhuri told me about god Krishna, in fact I was having very little knowledge about Hindu religion and gods at that time.

In January 1988 at the end of last semester of course work I was enjoying success had passed course work both semesters and was also preparing myself to write down thesis the topic of it was assigned to me as 'China as a factor in Pak-US relations' when I received a phone call from a senior running tourism firm in partnership with a German national Mr. Rudy un Islamabad capital of Pakistan.

Both have assigned me the task of being on protocol duty with two German elderly ladies of my Mom's age, their husbands were off for wild boar hunting and I was assigned to take away both ladies on a tour of Peshawar, Lahore and Karachi, salary package for me was excellent for that task my plane tickets and stay in five star hotels was also there as part of package. Had accomplished the task and had started working on my M Phil thesis. In August 1988 was informed by ASC director that I'll be part of students' delegation assigned to study US election campaign there.

Visit to USA

In September 1988 me along with my class fellow Farzana, Jamil Raza and Waheed Tariq came to USA to observe US election campaign, as promised by late US ambassador Raphael we were financed and sponsored by USIS Islamabad with prior approval of Director Area Study Center Dr. Iftikhar Haider Malik. US electoral system was quite fair; in 1988 in State of Nebraska polling was computerized. Unlike Pakistan in USA there was no Election Commission to conduct and regulate elections, states and local governments were responsible for making arrangements for polling and election results. We had visited Washington, New York, Nebraska, California and LA to observe and study US election campaign.

Washington in 1988 was quite a beautiful city, air pollution, especially smell of gas in the air was quite disturbing on highways, and our stay was in Du Pont Plaza. Library of congress, White House, and Capital Hills are worth seeing places there, women and men in Washington jog in their free time to shed extra weight and fats from their bodies, George Town and University there are quite romantic places of Washington.

During our four days stay in Washington we had met high ups of State department, had visited White House, Library of Congress, and Capitol Hills, during the evening in our free time we used to eat food in Indian restaurant Taj Mahal, which was quite expensive.

After completion of our scheduled meetings arranged by Visitor Program Service of USA in Washington, our next destination was New York. Our escort in USA Mr. James Bodner when we reached New York in September 1988 had placed us in a big Limousine car driven by an Italian driver, without his company we reached at the gate of Columbia University, the moment we came out from car a beauty queen of Quaid I Azam University Islamabad and a few badges senior from us known by her nick name Tipi appeared on a gate as a big and pleasant surprise for me and my three other class fellows, after exchange of formal words we requested her to guide us towards Columbia University hostel where we were bound to stay for one week.

Soon we were comfortably placed in a hostel room, a Pakistani foreign office employee and currently doing PhD in Columbia university came to pay us a visit an Indian female student Devika also came along with him, another university fellow of us living in New York had brought roasted chickens from a Pakistani restaurant in New York for us, within few hours we became familiar with the campus environment.

In the evening me and my other fellow visitor Mr. Jamil Raza came out from our hostel room to buy Pizza for our only female colleague Miss Farzana Muzafar and Mr. Waheed Tariq, and that funny incident occurred, while walking towards Pizza shop we both male colleagues unaware of New York culture were suddenly became alert when female students of Columbia university have started shouting while looking towards us 'gays, gays' I was already maintaining a safe distance from my male colleague I had further distanced myself from him, finally we have succeeded to buy Pizza, on the way back I was laughing at myself, in Pakistan where love making without formal marriage contract is crime and a culprit who do that without formal marriage contract is liable to receive 80 lashes on his back, and in case of a married man or woman if they got caught while making love with someone else other than their spouse are liable to be stoned to death, how can I even think about to have physical relations of sexual nature with any men or women, for rest of the week-long stay in the campus of Columbia University I was quite careful while coming out from my hostel room was keeping quite a safe distance from my male colleagues and was mostly trying to keep the company of female colleague just to avoid gay label on myself.

We had a detailed meeting with Academia of the University most memorable was meeting with blue eyed pipe smoking Chairman of Journalism department of Columbia University, the Chairman had enlightened us with his precious views, when we came out from his office life was having new meanings for all of us.

One another funny incident was occurred when Mr. James Bodner had asked me to look into the eyes of statue of goddess of wisdom installed in Columbia University campus, the saying is that after having eye contact with goddess of wisdom a person become wise, I looked into her eyes and then told Mr. Bodner Sir, she is a statue there is no harm in having eye contact with her, Mr. James Bodner was unaware of the fact that in Pakistani culture since my childhood I was trained to avoid eye contact with any female.

We had visited Liberty Island and paid homage to Statue of liberty, we had spent few hours their and again came back to New York in a ferry boat, while doing shopping a big surprise in New York for us was a sex shop, in Pakistan there is no concept of a sex shop we were quite amused to see artificial male sex organs of different shapes and sizes and artificial female dolls, neatly decorated and exhibited in shop.

Our next destination after New York was Lincoln Nebraska where we were eventually awarded with honorary citizenship by Secretary of Finance, Madam Vann Mahan and other citizens of state of Nebraska were quite nice and we had watched the presidential debate on TV jointly while sitting with notables of Nebraska at the residence of a family when in Lincoln Nebraska hosted a dinner in our honor.

We had reached California after brief stay in Lincoln Nebraska, where during our stay we had completed all our official commitments and at weekend had visited Nevada, from California at the last leg of our tour we had a brief stay in LA, meeting with Chairman of Political Science department Dr. Leo E Rose was quite interesting in Berkley campus, he was class fellow of Chairman Zulfikar Ali Bhutoo Shaheed, we were destined to have a trip to Hawaii for recreation but my class fellow Jamil Raza had insisted that we shall go to Bangkok instead of Hawaii, our scheduled was changed, while sitting in North West Airline plane I was sipping a tonic when plane start moving, it was our departure flight and I was relaxed after tense meetings during my 22 days stay in USA, the moment plane started catching speed on runway suddenly the plane was stopped, captain of the pilot announced that a huge hole in cockpit of the plane was recovered and passengers are saved from possible air crash, all the passenger will have overnight stay in LA the next day another plane will be arranged for the secure flight. We were accommodated in Holiday Inn for overnight stay, in the evening we had some fun in LA and next day we were heading towards Bangkok in North West Airlines plane.

At Tokyo airport we had a stay of six hours, immigration people had refused to allow us to move out from the airport, inside airport building, few snakes and a bowl of noodles was visible at the fast food restaurant, obviously I had to fast for next six hours, we Pakistanis can eat beef stakes in American restaurants and in USA we have Pakistani and Indian restaurants where we can eat food, but in Tokyo airport there was no other option available, during six hours inside Tokyo airport building while waiting for next flight towards Bangkok, I had seen many blonde and tall girls with Japanese features, these Japanese blondes were product of intermarriages between Japanese and Americans.

Eventually I and Jamil Raza were on our way towards Bangkok after spending six long hours in Tokyo airport while waiting for the next flight. Jamil Raza had bought few things from a shop in Tokyo airport but when we came out from Bangkok airport and had reached to hotel Jamil found his purchased items missing from his luggage, we had informed the airport authorities, but the authorities were unable to find out the missing goods.

On second story of hotel few yards away from my room swimming pool was there, we had to spend four days in Bangkok, to get rid of jet lag I jumped into swimming pool, soon two Thai girls came and started swimming around me in the pool, after half an hour swimming I was tired but fresh again. In the evening I had a massage in Thai massage parlor, was quite a good experience, many Americans and Saudi customers were there in the parlor, for only sixty dollars the massage facility was available, I enjoyed it a lot.

We had visited Sayam market in Bangkok to buy few necessities, after four days stay in Bangkok soon, we were on our way to Karachi, we had spent few hours at airport hotel in Karachi and eventually through a PIA flight had reached Islamabad.

Back in Pakistan

In 1990 I had accomplished M Phil, and had joined ASC for PhD, Dr. Sikander Hayat was supervisor of my M Phil thesis and he had also accepted to supervise my PhD thesis, but soon he was transferred as Education Attaché in USA, and I was left without supervisor. Interestingly during PhD our stipends were ended in result of new government policy in early 1990's, unlike USA in Pakistan university students are not encouraged to do jobs to meet their education expenses, QAU administration was bent upon throwing out those students from hostels, whom are engaged in any sort of part time job. In absence of my thesis supervisor Dr. Sikandar Hayat, it was useless to stay in the campus, I was called back home to Kohat,

My visit to Jalalabad Afghanistan

It was year 1991 Soviets were defeated in Afghanistan and a lawyer friend here in Kohat Barrister Wajeehudin was eager to visit Afghanistan to meet his friend Governor of Jalalabad Qadeerudin, he had asked for my company during his visit as journalist, I agreed and we three me, him and Adil had visited Jalalabad, the moment we crossed Torkham border from Peshawar in a high speed vehicle along with two guards, UN exhibited warnings started appearing on Torkham Jalalabad road regarding mines. The road was cleared from mines though till Jalalabad and not at a single spot we were stopped by militants for checking, scenery on both sides of the road was worth looking at, Afghan guard had told me this long black line on road side mountains is created by snake of Zahak, I replied to him if you people will dig this black line in mountains you will find diamonds in it, this long line is made of carbon, we reached safely

to the residence of Governor.

While Barrister Wajeehudin was in meeting with Governor Qadeerudin me and Adil was surrounded by

his palace guards out there at lawn, his guards had offered me Kalashnikov as gift which I politely refused

and had told them that I am a journalist my pen is more powerful than Kalashnikov. For lunch we came to

a hotel and in war torn city of Jalalabad I have seen extreme poverty and bullet holes in wooden doors of

shops and other buildings at mass scale.

While eating lunch in hotel we were surrounded by beautiful Afghan children wearing torn dresses and no

shoes, whatever money was there in my pocket I distributed among poor children of Jalalabad that day.

On way back we have seen Soviet tanks sunk in mud at the banks of river Kabul, such tanks were quite

big in number only their barrels were out from the mud, till evening we were safely back here in Kohat.

Marriage

Me and Sabahat were married to each other in consequence of decision taken by our families so it is a purely arranged marriage. Both my engagement and marriage with Sabahat came as surprise to me, I never knew her or heard about her.

I was in staff room of PAF College Kohat after teaching my students for three consecutive periods, when my colleague retired captain of Pakistan Army Sajid had informed me that soon you are going to be engaged and get married. When I reached home my Mom had informed me, I am going to marry you with daughter of my teacher colleague your aunt Mrs. Hafeeza Bashir Malik. Her daughter name is Sabahat and she is going to be your fiancé date of engagement is set and if you have any other girl in your mind forget her.

Whatever I am today is because of my Mom, my great father had his own shop and employees but he used to give all his income to my grandfather and was supporting his brothers and sister, all my education from Kohat Convent till QAU was financed by my Mom, as teacher and as principal of girls school she was having her own salary and pension after retirement, Rents from property owned by her was a big source of comfort for me, my two brothers and a sister,

I knew her decision about my marriage is final and refusal on my behalf will be source of further trauma related to pressure on me which I had experienced during period of my delayed acceptance, I agreed with my Mom and in a white house like palace owned by maternal uncle of Sabahat we both were declared engaged in presence of large number of guests there mostly from our families and family friends.

First wife of Sabahat's grandfather Malik Sharif was aunt of my father, after birth of Sabahat's father Malik Bashir she died, and Malik Sharif had opted for second marriage, he had six sons and daughter from his second wife, so Sabahat was having step uncles and aunt. Her father Malik Bashir after serving Pakistan Air Force had opted for service in Muscat and was declared brother of Sultan Qaboos and his trusted gift officer as well.

In year 1993 after two years of engagement finally our wedding date was set and I was called by mother in law to have a cup of tea with the family of Sabahat at their residence in Defense Kohat. And there in her home I had met her and her German Shepherd dog in presence of all family members. Soon we both got married, wedding dates, festivities and celebrations of me and Sabahat and her brother Faiz Malik and his wife Sobia were common.

In fifth year of marriage life I became father of my daughter Urooj, and soon after her birth I decided to leave the country for economic reasons, I was writing articles for English daily The Nation, went there to its head office in Islamabad and had met editor Butt sahib, when he came to know that I want to leave Pakistan he said in patriotic tone that if you will migrate to USA that will be great loss for Pakistan, work along with me in head office here I have got a job for you, a deputy secretary has vacated the seat of translator and you are hired to translate news for daily the Nation, remuneration was reasonable I agreed to accept his offer.

It was year 1999 and I was working as translator with daily the Nation in its Islamabad head office, my duty was to translate news for the Nation sent by correspondents for Urdu daily Nawai Waqt, both newspapers were owned by Nizami family I was there in newspaper office when had received a call from a captain of Pakistan Army, he was complaining about encirclement of Pakistan by India, President Clinton was US president at that time I had presented a written essay to Madam Cole the than US Cultural Secretary here in Pakistan in my essay I had highlighted services of Pakistan for USA as a cold war ally and had pleaded for US support for Pakistan in that difficult time.

Brother of Haji Manzoor Paracha, Saifoor Paracha was abducted in Kohat, press secretary of ex MNA Haji Javid Ibrahim Paracha, Awais had called me and had asked for more press so that authorities start taking interest in recovery of Saifoor Paracha from captivity of abductors, not only I had written and published his abduction story in daily the Nation but had also made phone calls to president of Pakistan for his early release, tribal areas of Pakistan at that time were domain of president of Pakistan, and president Muhammad Rafiq Tarar was father of my university senior and president of our IR department Society in QAU Muhammad Irfan Tarar. Soon Saifoor Paracha was released by his abductors.

At end of my first month newspaper administration had doubled my salary and had posted me in Lahore capital of Pakistan through a written letter, and then after an hour another letter was issued to me that my services are not required any more. I had three days stay in residence of Manzoor soil an ex librarian of American Center Islamabad, he and his friend Javid Siddiq editor of Nawai Waqt had introduced me to Managing Director Associated Press of Pakistan Javid Akhter, whom had posted me as part time Correspondent of APP in my home town Kohat.

I came back home here in Kohat and had started my job as part time correspondent of APP, became a member of Kohat press club, had won elections of the club, my opponent had got only one vote when polling results were announced, at oath taking ceremony of Kohat press club elected cabinet chief guest was Governor KPK Syed Iftikhar Hussain Shah, he had ordered construction of Kohat press club building near to his residence in KDA Kohat which was immediately constructed.

Had also started teaching US, British and Pakistan constitutions along with subject of International Law in law college here in Kohat, used to deliver lectures there on daily bases, was writing a column for English daily The Frontier Post and for daily The Nation as well, was appointed principal of college of education affiliated with Peshawar university and was also appointed VC of a private university as well, four jobs in colleges and part time job with APP along with writing columns for two English dailies and one Urdu weekly were enough to keep me busy. In a time span from 1998 till 2003 I became father of six children, twice twins came. During my tenure as principal of college of education and VC of a private university academic standards were raised and both academic institutions became financial stable as well. There was big rush of students' college of education was having only 100 seats, I had to place request before chancellor of Peshawar university for increase in number of seats, he was kind enough and had approved forty more seats for the college.

Jobs in UN projects

I was introduced to a Romanian Mr. Dragos Dino head of voter education section of UNOCRV project of Afghan presidential elections and his American colleagues by owner of weekly, all of them were here in Kohat to conduct polling for Afghan refugees residing here in KPK province of Pakistan. Their security head was retired captain Sarfaraz Khatak of Pakistan Army. I had joined them as Assistant Voter Education officer, the project was success, polls were conducted and Mr. Hamid Karzai became president of Afghanistan in consequence of 2004 elections.

My second job as protection officer in UNHCR sub project of FDMA in September 2011 till 31st December 2013 was about provision of protections to internally displaced people of tribal areas of Pakistan. In a same project I was posted as field officer and as Monitoring officer as well. I had monitored return of displaced people of Maidan area of Teerah was sent on deputation from Peshawar head office to Kohat for that purpose, my office in tent was established in Jerma facilitation center, the return of displaced people of Teerah went smoothly and they were sent back to their homes along with essential commodities provided to them by UNHCR and number of other nongovernmental organizations having tent offices in Jerma facilitation center of Kohat. I had made an effort to build Garrisons and police stations in tribal areas of Pakistan while responding to demands of tribal chiefs, eventually now tribal areas of Pakistan were merged as districts of Khyber Pakhtunkhwa province of Pakistan.

Prior to my both jobs in UN projects I was engaged as coordinator KPK in Canadian government funded project of a Pakistani NGO Governance Network International headed by Raja Naseem retired secretary of cabinet division. That project was about performance evaluation of various government departments of Pakistan.

Current status

I do contribute news stories and essays to Associated press of Pakistan as Part Time Correspondent and am based here in-home district of Kohat. Few last year ambassadors and diplomatic staff of thirty countries was were here in Kohat to attend spring festival arranged here by Pakistan Army in Church ground of Kohat, Associated Press of Pakistan and Interior ministry had called me to attend the festival, I had met ambassadors in Kohat Garrison club and have pleaded for promotion of peace during my conversations with them after dinner, had written complete report for APP afterwards.

Chief executive of groundreport.com Rachel Sterne has sold out her website, am not writing for that website any more, she had helped journalists around the globe to earn and express through her website, she is married now and having son to take care of while still based in New York.

Recently at wedding function an elderly retired professor had revealed that British colonial rulers have not paid anything to my family while building Garrison at our family lands in heart of Kohat city. I have decided to do some research to find facts, interestingly in encyclopedia Britannica no history of Garrison built in Kohat in year 1923 is available, have searched for more articles on this topic no traces of that period of history are found so far in which my family lands were taken away by British rulers to build garrison on it, I am planning to do some research about it in India Office Library in London, probably will be able to find complete facts regarding building of Kohat Garrison from record there.

Note: I had written my memoirs in response to the curiosity of my pro-democracy East European friend.